C000182835

To..........................

From...................

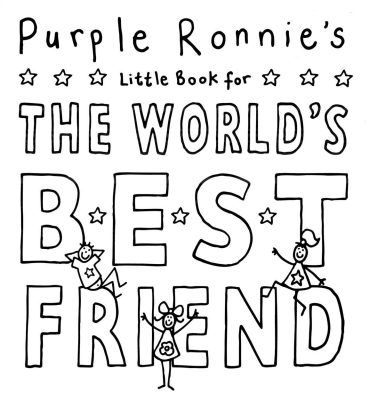

Purple Ronnie's
☆ ☆ ☆ Little Book for ☆ ☆ ☆
THE WORLD'S
BEST
FRIEND

First published 2010 by Boxtree
an imprint of Pan Macmillan, a division of Macmillan Publishers Limited
Pan Macmillan, 20 New Wharf Road, London N1 9RR
Basingstoke and Oxford
Associated companies throughout the world
www.panmacmillan.com

ISBN 978-0-7522-2723-8

Copyright © Purple Enterprises Ltd, a Coolabi company 2010

9 8 7 6 5 4 3 2 1

A CIP catalogue record for this book is
available from the British Library.

Printed and bound in Hong Kong

'Purple Ronnie' created by Giles Andreae. The right of Giles Andreae and Janet Cronin
to be identified respectively as the author and illustrator of this work has been asserted by them
in accordance with the Copyright, Designs and Patents Act 1988.

Visit www.panmacmillan.com to read more about all our books
and to buy them. You will also find features, author interviews and
news of any author events, and you can sign up for e-newsletters
so that you're always first to hear about our new releases.

a poem about

Fab Mates

When you're with your
girly friends
You don't have to be clever
Cos it's much more fun
just chatting
Or discussing men together!

blah blah...and the blue cup was next to the red cup!
I know, ...mmm, there there...

a poem about

Being There

You're there when I go on
and on
With all my _endless_ issues.
You're there with tea
and sympathy...
And thanks for all those
tissues

a poem to say you're

A Great Mate

Here's a special message
To tell you that you're great
You're an all time top
                    banana
And a really smashing mate

mate, you're the best
err... thanks... err...you too...
ALE
CIDER
bit embarrassed

Sometimes the best of friends have the worst arguments

a poem about a
Good Friend

Just because your girlfriend's
dumped you

Life's not going to end.

That's the time when I
step in

'Cos I'm your good old friend

a poem about

My Smashing Mate

You're chocolate cake and
soft ice-cream
Piled high upon my plate
You're a double jelly sandwich
dream
My splendid smashing mate

a poem about you being a

Lovely Person

You're always there to help me —
And I know you really care

So I wanted just to thank you
For always being there

A friend can come
in handy when you
have a job to do

a poem about

My Friend

I want to tell you something

It's soppy but it's true

If friendship grew like
flowers

I know that I'd pick YOU!

a poem about my
Great Friend

When things are really
                    hairy
And I'm going round the
                    bend
It's then I thank my lucky
                    stars
That you're my trusty friend

v. stressed
I can pay you tomorrow!
it'll be ok - let's go to the pub
broken
smoke
URGENT
BILL
LATE BILL
whiff
pong
cat poo

a poem about a

Special Friend

Whether we're together
Or whether we're apart

There's one place that you'll
always be
And that is...in my heart

Some friends are good
at giving advice.
While others are
just good at being
there

a poem about

You and Me

There's nothing like a gossip
And a glass of wine or two
But a bottle's so much better
When I'm sharing it with you!

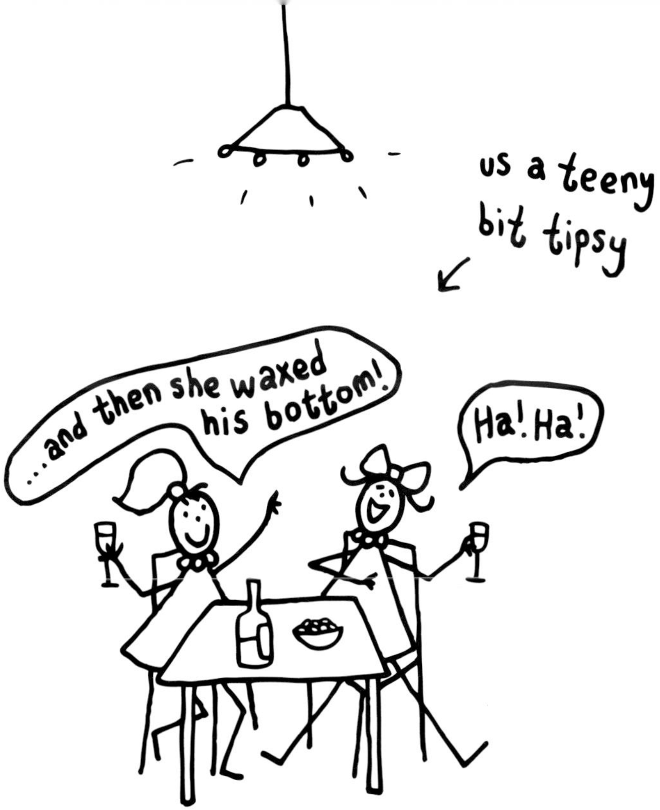
us a teeny bit tipsy
...and then she waxed his bottom!
Ha! Ha!

a poem about

Friends

Never think twice about
calling me up
To say that your pride has
been dented
To tell me you're happy or lonely
or sad
Cos that is why friends were
invented

a poem about

Man Friends

Fellers often aren't so
                    great

At telling tender feelings.

They're brilliant, though,
                at talking sport

And other blokey dealings

blah blah, yes mate, but that was off side blah
blah blah rubbish ref

Some people need
their friends to
be like THEM!

a poem about

Real Mates

Your pals will rally round
you
In a cheery, rowdy throng,
But a real mate will tell
you straight
When you are in the wrong

cringe
blush
you were well out of order there mate
too right!
shuffle

a poem about

Getting Home

When you've gotten plastered
And your face is on the
floor
A friend will somehow
get you home
'Cos that's what friends are
for!

Good evening officer
evenin' gentlemen
i'm a spaceman
hic
drag

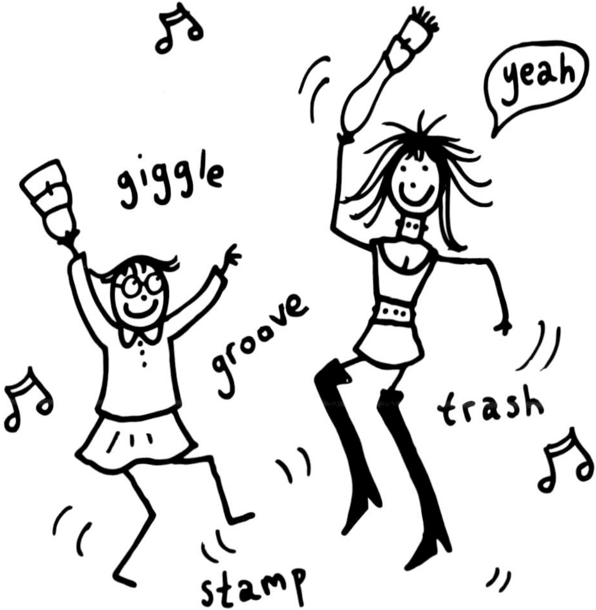
yeah
giggle
groove
trash
stamp

a poem about

Friendship

To be a friend, a person
doesn't have to be like
you,

Sometimes it's the difference

That makes the friendship
-glue

There's nothing like a quiet pint with a good mate

a poem about

Being Poorly

When you're sick and stuck
in bed
But getting on the mend,
That's the time you need
a visit
From a cheerful friend!

a poem about

Men Being Rubbish

It's men that are the
problem
They're often such dead
ends.
When men are being
bum heads
Thank God for women friends!

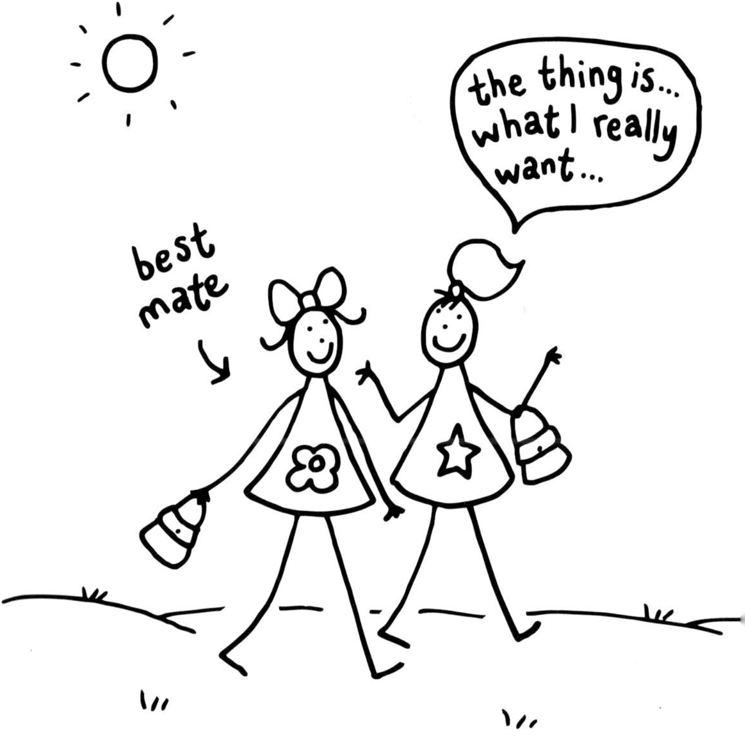
the thing is... what I really want...
best mate

a poem about

Close Friends

Lots of friends are
fabulous
For partying and fun
But when you're feeling
serious
It's time for One-to-One

Some people's best
friends are their pets

a poem about

Helpful Friends

When all the jobs are
mounting up,
With so much to be done,
If you can do them with
a friend
It's often much more fun!

a poem about

Friends and Family

When your family gets to you
And drives you nearly mad,
Remember you've got friends,
because
They're never half as bad!

a poem about

Never Being Lonely

It may look like I'm by
myself
I may look quite alone,
But all my friends are
with me
As I've got them on my
phone!

It's hard to have a
party without friends

a poem about

Man's Best Friend

If your pal is panting
And smelly at one end
Don't blame him, 'cos he's
just a dog

Which makes him...
Man's Best Friend!

a poem about

Great Friendship

I don't know why I like you

I guess that I just do

But I reckon I'd be lonely

Without my good friend

YOU !